THE
QUOTABLE
CAT

Jane Chambers

Illustrations by Henrietta Webb

CHARTWELL
BOOKS, INC.

First published in America
in 1995 by Chartwell Books,
a division of Book Sales Inc.,
by arrangement with Michael O'Mara Books Limited, London

Published by
CHARTWELL BOOKS, INC.
A Division of Book Sales, Inc.
114 Northfield Avenue
Edison, New Jersey 08837

ISBN 0-7858-0427-7

1 3 5 7 9 10 8 6 4 2

Designed by Mick Keates
Typesetting by Concise Artisans
Printed and bound in Hong Kong by Paramount Printing Group Ltd

INTRODUCTION

To err is human
To purr feline
ROBERT BYRNE

Napoleon feared them; Hemingway loved them; Steve Martin made fun of them; the Ancient Egyptians revered them as gods. Writers from James Herriot and T. S. Eliot to Mark Twain and Raymond Chandler were inspired by them – and the English language is rich in phrases, rhymes and sayings about them. 'The cat leaves a mark upon her friend,' as one old proverb says; and from the wildest alley-tom to the most cherished Persian, cats of all kinds have left their mark on human life and literature. Today, their recorded ways – and words – form a vast, and delightful, heritage of quotations.

This light-hearted new selection of feline wit and wisdom traces the communications between cats and people from ancient times to the present day. Some cat quotations are now popular classics, and this collection includes such favourites as P. G. Wodehouse who describes a cat called Webster as being an animal of 'deep reserves'; Kipling's haughty *The Cat That Walked by Himself*, and the immortal Cheshire Cat from *Alice in Wonderland*. Others, if less familiar, are no less revealing and the cat's love of luxury – along with its playfulness, independence and insatiable curiosity – have been recurring themes of cat-writing ever since.

The thoughts expressed in this book are those of movie-stars and Presidents; writers, and artists; cat-watchers famous and anonymous from every era. By turns amusing, touching or dramatic, they make a varied 'purr-pourri' – and together, add up to an affectionate tribute to that most quotable of animals, the Cat.

Girls are simply the prettiest things
My cat and I believe
And we're always saddened
When it's time for them to leave.

ROGER MCGOUGH

Female cats are very lascivious,
and make advances to the male.

ARISTOTLE

A cat belonging to M. Piccini has
assured us, that they who only know
how to *mew*, cannot be any judges
of the art of singing.

BENJAMIN FRANKLIN

Cats at firesides
live luxuriously
and are the picture
of comfort.

LEIGH HUNT

All cats love a cushioned couch.

THEOCRITUS

Something is going on right now
in Mexico that I happen to think
is cruelty to animals. I refer,
of course, to cat juggling.

STEVE MARTIN

Cats,
as a class,
have never
completely got over
the snootiness
caused by
the fact that
in Ancient Egypt
they were
worshipped
as gods.

P. G. WODEHOUSE

Macavity, Macavity,
there's no one like Macavity,
There never was a cat of such
deceitfulness and suavity.

T. S. ELIOT

You may have a cat in the room
with you without anxiety about
anything except eatables.
The presence of a cat is positively
soothing to a student.

PHILIP GILBERT HAMERTON

Cats too, with what silent
stealthiness, with what light steps
do they creep up to a bird!

PLINY THE ELDER

I love cats.
I even think we have
one at home.

EDWARD L. BURLINGAME

If you live with cats – or a cat –
you are less likely to have heart
trouble or high blood pressure.
Therefore, we who love them
and own them are really very
lucky indeed.

BERYL REID

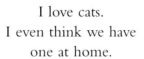

I had been concerned
for the loss of one of my cats
who had run away from me,
or, as I thought, had been dead,
and I heard no more tale or
tidings of her, till to my
astonishment, she came home
about the end of August with
three kittens.

DANIEL DEFOE

No matter how much
cats fight, there always
seems to be plenty of
kittens.

ABRAHAM LINCOLN

We brought with us in
the ship a cat, a most
amiable cat and greatly
loved by us; but he grew
to great bulk through
the eating of fish.

ST BRENDAN

Minnaloushe creeps through the grass
Alone, important and wise
And lifts to the changing moon
His changing eyes.

W. B. YEATS

Cats are not impure;
they keep watch
about us.

THE PROPHET MOHAMMED

I was only a small child when
the seeds of cat enchantment
were sown within me.

MAY EUSTACE

A common cat is
four legal pence in value…

A pound is the worth
of a pet animal
of the king.

HYWEL DDA

A cat I find…
is an easier companion
than a dog.

A cat's sense
of independence
also enables oneself
to be independent.

DEREK TANGYE

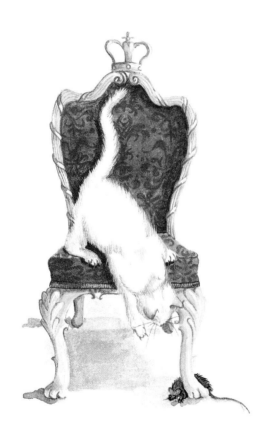

When he catches a mouse, he plays with it, and eats it after the play. And he is as it were wild and roams about at mating time. Among cats in time of love there is hard fighting for wives, and one will scratch and tear another grievously with biting and with claws.

BARTOLOMAEUS ANGLICUS

Cat lovers can readily
be identified.
Their clothes always look
old and well used.
Their sheets look like
bath towels and their
bath towels look like
a collection of knitting
mistakes.

ERIC GURNEY

A cat can climb down
from a tree
without the assistance
of the fire department
or any other agency.
The proof is that no one
has ever seen a cat skeleton
in a tree.

ANON

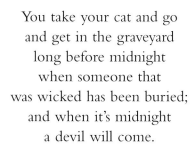

You take your cat and go
and get in the graveyard
long before midnight
when someone that
was wicked has been buried;
and when it's midnight
a devil will come.

MARK TWAIN

It is the nature of cats
to do a certain amount
of unescorted roaming.
The state of Illinois
and its governing bodies
have enough to do
without trying
to control feline
delinquency.

ADLAI STEVENSON

How come Kitty acts
not like the beast of prey
she is but like a better-
class human being?
I don't know the answer.
The point is she does it
– and makes you her slave
ever after.

PAUL GALLICO

What sort of philosophers
are we, that know
absolutely nothing of the
origins and destiny of cats?

HENRY THOREAU

There are cats and cats.

DÉNIS DIDEROT

'All right,' said the Cat;
and this time it vanished
quite slowly, beginning with
the end of the tail,
and ending with the grin,
which remained some time
after the rest of it had gone.
'Well! I've often seen a cat
without a grin,' thought Alice;
'but a grin without a cat!
It's the most curious thing
I ever saw in all my life!'

LEWIS CARROLL

When I play with my cat,
who can say whether she
is amusing herself with
me, or I with her?

MICHEL EYQUEM
MONTAIGNE

The poor Cat
had a dreadful stomach-ache,
and could only eat
thirty-five mullet
in tomato sauce,
and four helpings of tripe
garnished with
Parmesan cheese.

CARLO COLLODI

Children and cats in Venice
learn to swim almost as soon
as they learn to walk.

JOAN AIKEN

The city of cats
and the city of men
exist one inside
the other,
but they are not
the same city.

ITALO CALVINO

Once cats were all wild,
but afterwards they retired
to houses.

EDWARD TOPSELL

The Owl and the Pussy-cat went to sea,
In a beautiful pea-green boat,
They took some honey and plenty
of money
Wrapped up in a five-pound note.
The owl looked up to the stars above,
And sang to a small guitar,
'O lovely Pussy! O Pussy my love,
What a beautiful Pussy you are, you are,
What a beautiful Pussy you are!'

EDWARD LEAR

Some people say that cats
are sneaky, evil, and cruel.
True, and they have many
other fine qualities as well.

MISSY DIZICK

The crow is lame of leg –
wonder how it happened…
The falcon pretty brisk – the
cats large and noisy.

LORD BYRON

A cat has nine lives, and a
woman has nine cat's lives.

THOMAS FULLER

Lord Byron's establishment
consists, besides servants,
of ten horses, eight enormous
dogs, three monkeys, five cats,
an eagle, a crow and a falcon.

PERCY BYSSHE SHELLEY

Rescued a little kitten
that was perched in the sill of
the round window
at the sink over the gas-jet,
and dared not jump down…
I make a note of it
because of her gratitude.

GERARD MANLEY HOPKINS

Cats do not need
to be shown how to
have a good time,
for they are
unfailingly ingenious
in that respect.

James Mason

We have a black cat and
an old dog at the Rectory.
I know somebody to whose
knee that black cat loves to
climb; against whose
shoulder and cheeks it likes
to purr… And what does
that somebody do?
He quietly strokes the cat,
and lets her sit.

CHARLOTTE BRONTË

The best are such as are of a
fair and large kind, and of an
exquisite tabby colour.

WILLIAM SALMON

There was never a time
when our household did not
have several cats and they all
had their particular charm.
Their innate grace and
daintiness, and their deeply
responsive affection made
them all dear to me.

JAMES HERRIOT

Cats and monkeys,
monkeys and cats –
all human life is there.

HENRY JAMES

She would come home
in a shocking state, all bedraggled,
her fur so torn and dirty that
she had to spend a whole week
licking herself clean.
After that she would resume
her supercilious airs …
And one fine morning
she would be found
with a litter of kittens.

ÉMILE ZOLA

When the cat's away
the mice will play.

TRADITIONAL

The cat purrs to please himself.

TRADITIONAL

❧

Honest as a cat when food
is out of reach.

TRADITIONAL

❧

To err is human
To purr feline.

ROBERT BYRNE

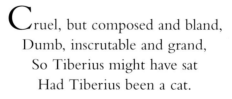

Cruel, but composed and bland,
Dumb, inscrutable and grand,
So Tiberius might have sat
Had Tiberius been a cat.

MATTHEW ARNOLD

Cats like men are flatterers.

WALTER SAVAGE LANDOR

All cats look grey in the dark.

TRADITIONAL

The most exquisite purr
I have known,
a real prima donna of a purr,
belongs to my own cat
'Four'!

BEVERLEY NICHOLS

The cat has nine lives –
three for playing,
three for straying,
three for staying.

ANON

Curiosity killed the cat.

TRADITIONAL

See the Kitten on the wall
Sporting with the leaves that fall,
Withered leaves-one-two-three
From the lofty elder tree!

WILLIAM WORDSWORTH

❧

Cats are a mysterious kind of folk.
There is more passing in their minds
than we are aware of.
SIR WALTER SCOTT

❧

To me a cat is just a waste of fur.

RITA RUDNER

When th'cat,
poor thing, jumped
onto his knee
he only stroked her,
and gave a bit of a smile:
so I thought that was
a good sign:
for once, when she
did so to th'Rector,
he knocked her off,
like as it might be in scorn
or anger, poor thing.
But you can't expect a cat
to know manners
like a Christian,
you know, Miss Grey.

ANNE BRONTË

Pussy cat, Pussy cat, where
have you been?
I've been to London to look at
the Queen.
Pussy cat, Pussy cat, what did
you there?
I frightened a little mouse
under her chair.

SONGS FOR THE NURSERY

Beware of those who dislike cats.

TRADITIONAL

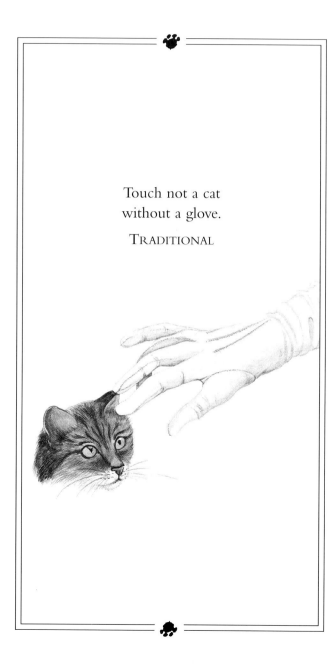

Touch not a cat
without a glove.

TRADITIONAL

Cats can be very funny,
and have the oddest ways
of showing they're
glad to see you.
Rudimac always peed
in our shoes.

W. H. AUDEN

When rats infest the Palace
a lame cat is better than
the swiftest horse.

CHINESE PROVERB

What stroke do cats use
when they swim?
The dog paddle.

DAVID TAYLOR

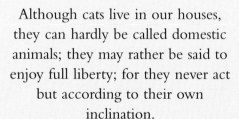

Although cats live in our houses,
they can hardly be called domestic
animals; they may rather be said to
enjoy full liberty; for they never act
but according to their own
inclination.

ENCYCLOPEDIA BRITANNICA

When I made the acquaintance
of Tobermory a week ago
I saw at once that
I was in contact with a
'Beyond-Cat' of
extraordinary intelligence.

'SAKI'

Do cats eat bats? …
Do bats eat cats?

LEWIS CARROLL

CAT: …
A domestic animal
that catches mice
commonly reckoned
by naturalists the
lowest order of
leonine species.

SAMUEL JOHNSON

A Cat May Look At A King

TITLE OF A POLITICAL
PAMPHLET

'You don't mean to say
there's an Invisible Cat
at large in the world?'
said Kemp.

H. G. WELLS

Like the rest of the nobility,
she is much given
to hunting, birding
and fishing, but hates all
other sorts of exertion.

THOMAS BROWN

Cat said, 'I am not a friend
and I am not a servant.
I am the Cat who walks
by himself.

RUDYARD KIPLING

I had tacked it together
(and the beauty of this fine lace is
that, when it is wet, it goes into
a very little space), and put it to
soak in milk… On my return
I found pussy on the table, looking
very like a thief, but gulping very
uncomfortably… all at once
I looked and saw the cup of milk
empty – cleaned out!

ELIZABETH GASKELL

The only subject on which
Montmorency and I have
any serious difference of
opinion is cats. I like cats;
Montmorency does not.

JEROME K. JEROME

Mrs Pipchin had an
old black cat, who generally
lay coiled upon the centre
foot of the fender, purring
egotistically, and winking
at the fire.

CHARLES DICKENS

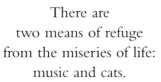

There are
two means of refuge
from the miseries of life:
music and cats.

ALBERT SCHWEITZER

Cat on a hot tin roof.

TENNESSEE WILLIAMS

Cats, like owls,
see best in the dark.
They go best a-mousing
in the dark, and
may prefer the dark
for their private, social and
even public affairs.

WALTER DE LA MARE

The most domestic cat,
which has lain on a rug
all her days, appears quite at
home in the woods.

HENRY THOREAU

Perhaps a child, like a cat,
is so much inside of himself
that he does not see himself
in the mirror.

ANAÏS NIN

There were people who said
it was dangerous to leave a cat
with a baby… The most
ignorant and prejudiced
said that a cat would
suck a baby's breath
and kill him.

ERNEST HEMINGWAY

Few animals display their mood via facial expressions as distinctly as the cat.

KONRAD LORENZ

People who belong to Siamese
cats must make up their minds
to do a good deal of waiting
upon them.

COMPTON MACKENZIE

She scratches her neck
with a foot of rapid delight,
leaning her head towards it, and
shutting her eyes,
half to accommodate
the action of the skin,
and half to enjoy the luxury.

J. H. LEIGH HUNT

All dogs look up to you.
All cats look down to you.

WINSTON CHURCHILL

He laughed at cats –
until they robbed him
of wealth, health
and reason.

EPITAPH FOR LOUIS WAIN

The Cat is a guest and
not a plaything.

COLETTE

Webster was very large
and very black
and very composed.
He conveyed
the impression of
being a cat
of deep reserves.

P. G. WODEHOUSE

Once upon a time
there were three little kittens,
and their names were
Mittens, Tom Kitten and Moppet.

BEATRIX POTTER

In October not even a cat
is to be found in London.

ANON

Casper seems to defy
the rules of nature,
well, at least cat nature,
with his aquatic tendencies.
I think he's really a catfish.

JEAN CANFIELD

There was a crooked man,
and he went a crooked mile
He found a crooked sixpence
against a crooked stile
He bought a crooked cat,
which caught a crooked mouse
And they all lived together
in a little crooked house.

NURSERY RHYME

'The feline species is
as abhorrent to me as it was
to the great Napoleon.
Contact with it destroys
my nerve entirely!'
'What's he mean?'
whispered William
to his neighbour.
'He means he don't like cats,'
said William's neighbour.
'Well, why don't he say so then?'
said William scornfully.

RICHMAL CROMPTON

It was soon noticed that when
there was work to be done the
cat could never be found.

GEORGE ORWELL